PRAISE FOR

I ASK ABOUT WHAT FALLS AWAY

I ask about what falls away is a love letter in a time of "divine sorrow"....
Razed lands, the rise of militarization, targeted state violence—the
vortex of violence in these times can drain us of hope and imagination,
and yet, here is where Perez's work delivers us an antidote to despair,
what he calls "the recklessness of / memory, the autonomy of sorrow, /
& these counter-narratives of joy." This book invents a grammar of care,
linking the anti-colonial wisdom of Neferti X. M. Tadiar to Aimé Césaire,
Claudia Rankine to Susan F. Quimpo, scholar-poet to ate, a network of
citational abundance to counter the exploitative language of capitalist
disposability, each refrain a demonstration of radical remembrance and
connection beyond mourning—what stays, what keeps.
— MURIEL LEUNG, author of *Imagine Us, the Swarm*

...Jason Magabo Perez's compelling book is a timely, lyrical balm where
his beloved city becomes a site of activism and hope...Here, Perez
provides us this language of survival, electric with protest and tender
lamentation.
—ANGELA PEÑAREDONDO, author of *nature felt but never apprehended*

[P]henomenal. If [*I ask about what falls away*] was an album, I'd have
it on repeat. Here, in stunning pieces that move with agility between
expansiveness and distillation, litany and [the] granular, Jason Magabo
Perez undertakes a sustained act of attention that speaks us closer to
ourselves, closer to our full capacity for listening, grief, creativity—[clos-
er to] living at all.... Here, the "inconsequential scene" offers [both] past
and future, [a]... threshold that resists tourism... Here there is "longing
beneath rebellion"—shoelaces, pillow forts, the homies, the elders...
enacting the difficult crucial work of "what is ghost, what is bone, what
is subject." In reading this book, I'm seriously, joyfully transformed. *I ask
about what falls away* does nothing less than shift the way I attend to
my own memory and imagination. I wish this for you.
—HARI ALLURI, author of *Our Echo of Sudden Mercy*

In Jason Magabo Perez's *I ask about what falls away*, the poet indexes the relentlessness of life and death under coloniality: there is grief, sorrow, rage, and the material conditions under which they emerge. But there is also the Filipinx working-class life that vibrantly refuses to slip through the cracks of crisis, carefully marked through language without easily being given away... When Perez writes, "you & I desire nothing short of the unthinkable," he reminds me that poetry is a social place where the process of liberation can be not only imagined, but actively practiced toward reality. Let the fierce and tender stream of his language carry you into the work of that doing.
—MARYAM IVETTE PARHIZKAR, author of *Somewhere Else the Sun is Falling into Someone's Eyes*

I ASK ABOUT WHAT FALLS AWAY

—

JASON MAGABO PEREZ

Distributed by D.A.P./Distributed Art Publishers // artbook.com (800) 388-BOOK
ISBN: 9781885030894
Library of Congress Control Number: 2023952622
Cover artwork by Matt Manalo
Book design by Chez Bryan Ong (www.spoonandforkstudio.com)

This publication is made possible by support from the USC Dana and David Dornsife College
of Arts, Letters, and Sciences; and the USC Department of American Studies and Ethnicity.
Special thanks to Stephen CuUnjieng and the Choi Chang Soo Foundation for their support of
this work.

Additional funding was provided by generous contributions from: Tanzila Ahmed, Chitra Ai
yar, Chantal Rei Alberto, Sasha Ali, Hari Alluri, Heidi Amin-Hong, Stine An, Akhila Ananth, Tif-
fany Babb, Manibha Banerjee, Neelanjana Banerjee, Terry Bequette, Hung Bui, Cari Campbell,
Emiliana Chan, Susan Chan, Sam Chanse, Alexander Chee, Anelise Chen, Anita Chen, Dehua
Chen, Jean Chen, Lisa Chen, Floyd Cheung, Jayne Cho, Jennifer Chou, Yvonne Chow, Caroline
Chow, Elizabeth Clemants, Tuyet Cong Ton Nu, Herna Cruz, Timothy Daley, Lawrence-Minh
Bui Davis, Glenda Denniston, Susannah Donahue, Taiyo Ebato, Irving Eng, Matthew Fargo, Pe-
ter Feng, Sia Figiel, Sesshu Foster, Sylvana Freyberg, Diane Fujii, Joseph Goetz, K A Hashimoto,
Jean Ho, Ann Holler, Huy Hong, Jacqueline Hoyt, Lisa Hsia, Jonathan Hugo, Adria Imada, Susan
Ito, Ashaki Jackson, Carren Jao, Mia Kang, Andrew Kebo, Vandana Khanna, Nidhi Khurana,
Seema Khurana, Swati Khurana, Joonie Kim, Seonglim Kim, Gwendolyn Knight, Sabrina Ko,
Timothy Ko, Robin Koda, Juliana Koo, Sun Hee Koo, Rika Koreeda, Emily Kuhlmann, Eileen Ku-
rahashi, Paul Lai, Jenny Lam, Iris Law, Samantha Le, Catherine Lee, Helen Kim Lee, Hyunjung
Lee, Marie Myung-Ok Lee, Stacy Lee, Whakyung Lee in memory of Sonya Choi Lee, KC Lehman,
Edward Lin, Carleen Liu, Veronica Liu, Mimi Lok, Andrea Louie, Pauline Lu, Haline Ly, Abir
Majumdar, Jason McCall, Sally McWilliams, Sean Miura, Faisal Mohyuddin, Greg Monaco,
Russell Morse, Adam Muto, Wendy Lou Nakao, Jean Young Naylor, Kim Nguyen, Kathy Nguyen,
Viet Thanh Nguyen, Vinh Nguyen, erin ninh, Dawn Oh, Julia Oh, Eric Ong, Tiffany Ong, Camille
Patrao, Thuy Phan, Cheryline Prestolino, James Pumarada, Jhani Randhawa, Amarnath Ravva,
Maria L Sandoval, Nitasha Sawhney, Carol Say, Andrew Shih, Brandon Shimoda, Luisa Smith,
Roch Smith, Jungmi Son, daniela sow, Nancy Starbuck, Karen Su, Rachana Sukhadia, Robin
Sukhadia, Rajen Sukhadia, Kelly Sutherland, Willie Tan, Zhen Teng, Wendy Tokuda, Frederick
Tran, Monique Truong, Patricia Wakida, Dan S. Wang, Aviva Weiner, Duncan Williams, Wil-
liam Wong, Amelia Wu and Sachin Adarkar, Anita Wu and James Spicer, Stan Yogi, Kyung Yoon,
Shinae Yoon, Mikoto Yoshida, Patricia Yun, and many others.

Kaya Press is also supported, in part, by the National Endowment for the Arts; the Los
Angeles County Board of Supervisors through the Los Angeles County Arts Commission; the
Community of Literary Magazines and Presses and the Literary Arts Emergency Fund; and the
City of Los Angeles Department of Cultural Affairs.

Special thanks to Kaitlin Hsu and Austin Nguyen for their work on this book.

I ASK ABOUT WHAT FALLS AWAY

—

JASON MAGABO PEREZ

KAYA
PRESS

for B.P. Benito

aka B-Boy
aka Buwisit
aka B

(1977–2019)

Temporality is cleft between a time of history and times of waste.

— NEFERTI X. M. TADIAR

call this raw material literature

call this principled surrender

call this grammar of worry

I draft this, dear kasama, against
fish-hooks of hope. I draft against
slow elimination. I draft from soft
interior of riot. I draft syllables
of known sadness, such knowing,
such evidence, such kitchen table
phenomenology of you reading
this, of this reading you—on a rainy
morning, I see you, through the
window, in a blue mask & black
hoodie, delivering bags of groceries
at the doorstep. I draft from collected
stillness, restless ghosts archived
in my veins. Consider this an intimate
poetics of rage. Consider this rage
divine refusal. Let us talk about such
refusal. Let us talk about such
dysregulation of promise. Let us
talk about how much I miss you.

Drive east on University toward 49th.
Park your Civic in the alley out back.
This alley of splendor & solitude—
a gallery of rain-soaked mattresses. A
child will slide down a half-assembled
red plastic slide into a small hill of
middle grade paperbacks. You'll find
a gold purse filled with fresh broccoli
& blue rubber gloves. You'll find

prayer at daybreak. This alley will smell
of dank weed & brake dust. You'll find
on the ground a black tote bag stuffed
with wet lettuce & white surgical masks.
It'll seem like this was dropped in a hurry.
You'll wonder if that hurried person is safe.
You'll notice a wire fence across the alley
limp as days go by. Swarms of flies will
hover above plastic trash bins. Crows
will cross the alley. Someone will keep
claiming the telephone pole in blue spray-
painted letters you'll never be able to decipher.
Someone will be barbecuing carnitas y elote.
On sunny days, dried lemon rinds will stick
hard to pavement. One day, in front of your
Civic, you'll find cleaned chicken bone
wrapped in foil. Neighbors on the other end will
party. You'll hear bottles clanking. Patrol
cars will cram the alley for no good reason.
& it'll smell of burnt plastic & cigarette smoke.
You'll hear sirens. You'll hear laughter. You'll
hear water drumming against trash bags full of
aluminum cans. This will be an afterparty for
afterlives. An elder neighbor will warn you of
drugs & the devil's work. A crew of youth will
hotbox an old Pathfinder. On the rainiest days,
this alley will be a shallow river—weeds, shreds
of paper, crow feathers, & dried lemon rinds
rushing downstream. Someone will break into
your Civic. Someone will break into your Civic
again. They will steal neither your surplus
of Starbucks napkins nor your prized
Blackstreet CDs. They will steal some old

prescription eyeglasses & a broken pair of
headphones. Yes, & there'll be The Homie.
Quiet, please—The Homie will be sound
asleep on that perfectly fine, barely faded,
but discarded wooden dining chair. When
you see The Homie, please leave masks. Please
leave bottled water. Please leave bags of ice.
Please leave a hot carne asada burrito. &
please leave two toothbrushes, one for The
Homie's teeth, & one for The Homie's Jordan 1s.
Place everything in plastic bags. Hang the bags
gently on the handlebars of The Homie's BMX...
Shhhhhhhhhhh.

this sadness	is a politics
this sadness	knows
this sadness	holds
this sadness	wants
	warns
	warms
sadness	in the shadow of capital
sadness	against white supremacy
sadness	against imperialism
sadness	against tanks & tear gas
sadness	blocking killer-cop kneecap near neck
sadness	that in fact is its own godforsaken solidarity statement

if you want to know what we are—

melodramatic telenovela	sadness
bulletproof	sadness
clap-back	sadness
confessional	sadness
abomunist	sadness
anticolonial	sadness

say say land back say say all power to the people say say I am the
people say say I am not the pig say say makibaka say say makibaka say
say junk Anti-Terror Law say say demilitarize say say deoccupy say say
para todos todo say say la lucha se sigue say say hasta la victoria say
say huwag matakot say say isulong say say ingat say say isang bagsak
say say sadness

sadness	of my mother's & father's return from home to here—what could be a final return
sadness	of departures
sadness	of colonial removal
sadness	of perpetual displacement
such sadness	is so Filipino
such sadness	is relational urgency
such sadness	is abolitionist sadness
such sadness	is quotidian sadness

after the graveyard shift
Black & brown nurses in
grey & pink scrubs wait
together at Valerio's City Bakery
to order silogs & catering
    & some of us overtheorize solidarity
in the middle of East 8th
large crows swoop on the carcass
of an adorable dead possum &
across the street I see
His & Hairs Barber Shop
& I believe whoever named
this business should win the most
prestigious of literary awards
& somewhere at work
your wrists & your lungs
ache & your neck cramps
& you may be coughing
& coughing & weak with fever
    all inside this throb this
    rot of racial capitalism

Honor the longing beneath rebellion.
Seven shots of bourbon. Consider

this emergence: my asthmatic lungs
approximate candid disaster, unrelieved

ruin of verb & vein. There goes our
Bisayan postal worker with notice of

deathbreak, a commuting of temporalities.
In proximal distance between throat &

line break is promise of cut-up song,
bookish banter, memorial for those

unmapped, those unmentioned. Between
chest & gesture hums fracture & fractal.

Sleep, sleep longing, sleep cold, sleep
mythos. Outside this taqueria: raw

chicken skin on sidewalk, & this child
chasing mosquitos with a hammer.

Imagine the honesty of the dead. Imagine it
pressing. Imagine water inside what gets
remembered, what gets remembered inside
the pinkish grey glow of an uncle's surgery
scar, what scars from a life of being worked.
This calm in excess of crisis. In the backyard,
on the folding table, rests a round tupperware of
buko salad. There fly langaw langaw everywhere
everywhere. These sorts of things migrate. These
sorts of things thesis. These things make mess,
an artist's guide: a queer genealogy going &
going & going. Such mourning is discontinuous,
& there goes uncle in a Sunday white Lakers jersey
& gold watch & gold chain, & there goes auntie
in a purple & gold swapmeet Starters jacket,
& there goes another auntie protecting the
buko salad with a hospital blue shower cap.

I hope this finds you well.
I hope this finds you well & thriving.
I hope this finds you in the goodness of things.
I hope this finds you in good health.
I hope this finds you in good health & in good spirits.
I hope this finds you in the way it needs to find you.
I hope this finds you in the way you need to find it.
I hope this finds you.

·

I no longer have grey dress pants that fit.

On the morning of B's funeral, I am simply unwilling.

The only funeral shoes I have are ratty brown Oxfords with blue
shoelaces.

So I rush to CVS to grab black shoelaces.

I browse to feel something.

Should I get athletic shoelaces? Fat laces? Rope laces?

What is the normative length for shoelaces?

Should I just get long ones?

What if they're too long?

I end up with long ones.

Back home, I relace my Oxfords & snip off the eyelets.

Here I am with snipped laces that might fray at any moment.

At Good Shephard, the priest says we grieve persons, but we also grieve
    places.

The priest will never know how much I miss Mira Mesa.

The priest will never know how I refuse to describe B here for B's sake.

The priest will never know how loud we bumped Sean Paul's "Gimme
    the Light" in the ICU during B's last hours.

Who knows how many months this grey overcoat, this white shirt, this
    black tie, these black socks, these unhemmed grey dress pants will
    hide at bottom of the hamper after all this?

& yes I still wonder about each kind of heaven.

For now, we're on this familiar hill at El Camino Memorial.

& there sinks slowly into its plot B's casket.

& I wonder if one can actually own one's own casket.

& I cannot for the life of me know what will exceed this or what will
    remain.

How ridiculous my shoelaces look!

How ridiculous the genre of funeral shoes!

We carry barely enough gospel for another time.

I imagine
you so

far along
this sentence,

somewhere beyond
city, beyond

this breath
of inexhaustible

thought, where
grass burns.

Follow us,
kasama, far

under. Follow
us, kasama,

communion of
magic, barrel

of possibility.
Let poetics

need less
ideology, a

future so
radically clumsy.

Then all life is a form of waiting, but it is the waiting of loneliness.

— CLAUDIA RANKINE

Here, inside of this sentence—stretching toward the Pacific, set deep, here, in the thick historical present, out front of a foreclosed single-family home, past a dried-dead yellow lawn, past plastic-covered furniture of the evicted, out front of a one-bedroom apartment, each wall lined with bunk beds for migrants since long ago, here, out front of another out-of-business

Filipino restaurant, here, along a sidewalk of discarded shoelaces, receipts, &

grocery lists, here, on the corner of Black Mountain & Mira Mesa, the smell of beef broth & basil & gasoline & turmeric & cilantro & fresh asphalt & deep–

fried rice paper, here, at the bus stop with students, tech workers, lolas y abuelitas in straw sun hats & visors, their reused plastic Target bags sagging with bleached white socks & the salvaged of yesterday's chichiria, here, where many un-English languages are familiar music, familiar longing, familiar refusal, a tin & garlic glottal syllable every now & again, here, now at this very bus stop, amidst the screech of brakes & the hum of traffic, here, in all of these clauses, lives, so quietly, so humbly, at the helm of divine laughter, this unremarkable man, his brownness an archipelago of eczema & radiation pink, his nailbeds tinted chemical green, his oversized blue & orange

Pendleton full of single threads running & running, his unevenly hemmed groundskeeper khakis consistently starched, his Florsheim loafers freshly polished, Solvang cap still stiff on his head, still stained with coffee & brandy, his same spectacles bent, resting crooked & uneasy, here: a labor of a man, who at the end of this sentence, this mourning, this story, shall be remembered simply as pare, amigo, kasama, compa, lolo, asawa, tatay, tito, tío, uncle, manong, abalayan, stranger, ninong, labor, that widower who could never petition his familia, that sometimes lettuce-picker, sometimes strawberry-picker, laid-off bellhop, laid-off postal worker, freelance maintenance worker, freelance custodian, retired grounds-keeper, comrade who plays chess & waxes geographic with fellow elders at the sacred Starbucks on Camino

Ruiz, that 82-year-old who when diagnosed with walking pneumonia again

& again this whole past year eventually for one last time stops by Seafood City to scarf down the saltiest of dilis, who drinks a six-pack of Red Horse & cries through his throat, who boards the bus, & sings for the dead at every streetlight altar along the boulevard, who travels down the 805, to La Jolla Village

Drive, where he once went on strike at the Marriott, where he once at the bar fantasized about rushing a white man for calling him stupid & dirty down to the VA hospital, here, now, he smokes a handful of Reds, & hikes down the hill, passes archways, condos, & mansions where wealthy white people live, where university chancellors live above bones of indigenous people, down to La

Jolla Shores, across grass, into sand, past college kids drinking cheap vodka in water bottles, past weakly lit bonfires, that laky who at this moment remembers then forgets who he is, what is ghost, what is bone, what is subject, he is migrating again, this old man who for this one last time shall remember then forget his name, his song, lyrics aflame & escaping through cracks in his lungs, this lolo who disrobes himself one final time of that pressed Pendleton

& those starched khakis, this lolo who, here, now is walking & whistling along the shore, still in white briefs, white socks, Solvang cap, & bent spectacles, this lakay, whose skin is quickly becoming all scales, who is walking &

whistling into the waves further & further until he needs to tread, then swim, &

now he is swimming & swimming, & his arms become fins, his legs twist into a thick tail, his walking pneumonia no longer, canals of water in his lungs no longer, no longer cracks in his breath, or his throat, or his lungs, or his song, his body now gills all over, now there, all the way over there, beyond this, beyond this sentence, is that lakay, his body now bursting &

bursting so full of the Pacific—

As expansive as its movement might be, divine sor-row always builds on and remains tied to a relation of intimacy—a friend, a loved one, a people whose fate one shares, whose suffering spells one's own.

— NEFERTI X. M. TADIAR

There is so much to say of this
mighty quiet. Let us begin here
in murk of struggle, a manuscript

is but scraps of notebook paper
smuggled into prison cell, into
forever, wherever there is deep

listening, wherever we are
waist-high in river, wherever a
marxism fumbles out of my

mouth, wherever the river mouths
a psalm, wherever that psalm is
glass bottle, gasoline, cloth,

flame exploding on government
walls. Gutter stream is context for fish
trapped in net, sugar trapped in blood,

blood & children rushing downstream,
down this very street. This sacrifice: body
of carabao halved, its hooves tender

on asphalt, a weeping, a sobbing, a
yearning—smallest of axes hacking
sky then flesh, hacking flesh then

sky. We wade again in another river.
Wherever we slip on tiny stones,
wherever a small mound is too

steep, wherever our syllabus wars
against sword & scripture, wherever we
crawl through windpipe of mountain,

hike in a cave of bats, dip in dark water
glorious. You—on a beach elsewhere,
sustained in hymn & footnote

somewhere. Let's steep these
Sagada tea leaves longer than usual.
Let's be the explicit trouble of study,

the specific praxis of monkey dance,
of biting black, gold, & red tinalak.
Wherever ancestors smell a lit match,

hear the cool of acoustic, historical
reckoning in the expanse of lung. This
loss is but a harvesting of the dreamt,

a vastness of rice terrace:
perspiring shamans, their teeth dark
red from betel nut, humming literatures

for the wild boar departing—meat for
the estranged. There is salt, uncertainty,
& plastic cups of Red Horse. Strum

guitar—this is a mighty quiet for you,
sister of salvaged young, mothering &
mothering many of us: on a humid evening,

you say my life's work is to write
the history of my mother, the hurt
made anthem. Wherever there is

so much song, so much promise, so
much to say of this mighty quiet:

let us ask about savage
let us ask about salvaged
let us ask about surplussed

let us ask about remaindered
let us ask about monstrous
let us ask about fugitive

let us ask about excess
let us ask about haunted
let us ask about hunted

let us ask about precarious
let us ask about unmapped
let us ask about unprotected

let us ask about mostless
let us ask about underfuture

our lady of lived refusal

our lady of irregular showers

our lady of isang bagsak

our lady of barber shops & hair salons

our lady of anti-capitalism

our lady of leftover menudo

our lady of decolonization

our lady of albuterol inhaler refills

our lady of abolition

our lady of loud-ass neighbors

our lady of autonomy

our lady of Filipino spaghetti

our lady of solidarity

our lady of Black youth pirouetting out front

I return to this inconsequential scene as I think of the eldest uncle.

The scene is simple.

We're outside a family party.

It's incredibly sunny but cold.

The youngest uncle's van pulls up.

The youngest uncle helps a middle uncle into his wheelchair.

Sadly, about a year from this seemingly inconsequential scene, this
middle uncle in the wheelchair will die of complications from ALS.

In this moment, in this distillation, the eldest uncle walks up to the van
to greet his younger brothers.

The eldest uncle removes his blue Solvang trucker cap & salutes both other uncles.

The eldest uncle untucks & lifts his white polo shirt & reveals a long pinkish grey heart surgery scar across his chest.

No words, no English, just the scar.

Years after the middle uncle in the wheelchair dies, the eldest uncle's health, too, will begin to deteriorate.

The eldest uncle's dementia will become hard to manage.

The eldest uncle's health will become a topic of discussion at family parties.

It'll prove too difficult for the eldest uncle's wife, our auntie, to serve as primary caregiver.

& assisted living, regretfully, will be too expensive.

So, regretfully, the eldest uncle, a retired hospital custodian, & auntie, a caregiver & seasonal strawberry-picker, will migrate back to the Philippines.

& we will mourn the fact that the family is separating slowly once again—migrating home, migrating toward death.

While home, the eldest uncle will stop taking his medications.

Soon after, somewhere between Bulacan & Pangasinan, the eldest uncle will go missing.

It will be difficult for all other uncles & aunties to find the eldest uncle.

One morning, one auntie texts us a picture—proof that the eldest uncle has been located & is safe & okay.

Weeks later, the eldest uncle falls ill & dies.

We never give ourselves appropriate time & space to grieve.

One day, at a university library, I'll start drafting a fiction about the eldest uncle's final day in which he turns into a fish.

I'll imagine the eldest uncle washing pots & pans in the bathtub.

Students will be studying & I'll fade in & out of sleep.

I'll reflect on what it means that the eldest uncle was the last one to migrate to the States, but the first one to migrate back to the Philippines, not the first one to die, but most definitely the first one to die at home.

I'll click the library desk lamp on & off with the hope of finding inspiration to narrate a sentence that never ends.

But this will be years from the inconsequential scene described above.

For now, at this point, in this distillation, the eldest uncle, his wife, our auntie, the youngest uncle with the van, the middle uncle in the wheelchair, & all the other aunties & uncles, except one—a middle uncle who joined the Navy & petitioned all the other aunties & uncles to get here—are still alive.

Forgive me, please, for wanting to live inside this distillation, this inconsequential scene, this moment just before another family party, for just a little while longer.

trauma-informed syllabus
trauma-informed settlement
trauma-informed colonialism
trauma-informed capitalism
trauma-informed neoliberalism
trauma-informed university
trauma-informed diversity
trauma-informed equity
trauma-informed inclusion
trauma-informed wage theft
trauma-informed prisons
trauma-informed policing
trauma-informed pandemic
trauma-informed English

What remains is a temple of internalized
rupture. What remains are scraps of
syntax. What remains is vulnerable to
wage theft. I sing against profit. I sing
lost against return. I sing estimated
antagonisms. I sing an accumulation
of need. For what is blessing but
bluff, bluff but confusion, a weight of need
versus a weight of disrepair. All that is
different should madden, should thrill.
This dead smell. This river of dank. This
nonserious kinship of isolation. There is
something gentle in rethinking revolution
itself, in shrapnel of afterlife, in the disposability
of heartbreak, in vinegar of paranoia. In
workshop, I sing as replaced tenant against
hello, against the march of history, with
cranial guitar strings strummed hella hella hella.

I give you this labored
breathing. I give you
wreckage from material
joy. I give you miracle of
collapsed rapture. I think
of my cousin who works
as a crying lady. Each day,
they wake up to perform
a mourning for wealthy
strangers. Each day,

a fetishization,
a performance,
a transaction
of sorrow.

Fish archive for
poetics. Fish strange
intimacies as archive
of war. Fish for
rhythm of suffering.
I know this mourning
to be chaotic. What I
could tell you right now
is simply a ghost of
what I need right now.

I ask for your tenderness,
in which redundancy collects
figures in search of the wept,
figures in search of those violated
by the angel of history. Figures who
remain non-propertied. Figures who
need no permission for this savage
alley-speak, for these bodies of want.
Tell me of current pleasures. Tell me
of our drives from Chula Vista back
to City Heights. Tell me we will always
pass the uncles gathering joyously at
midnight outside the Somali restaurant
beside the banh mi shop. Tell me this is
beyond capital. Tell me of a war
on property. These blocks are still blue
hot: As we wait, gunfire erupts on
Menlo just south of El Cajon,
a few blocks east of Hoover High;
as we wait, every death hurts;
as we wait, 20 to 25 gunshots;
as we wait, SWAT blocks the intersection
at University & Euclid; as we wait,
every exonerated cop, every security guard,
every white supremacist vigilante; as we wait,
officers shoot & kill a homicide suspect.
As we wait, we refuse the language policing

this city, the language endangering these families.
No matter the redirection of traffic these days,
no matter whose blood on the scene, this is state
violence. No matter the gentle rumination—
we stay fish in a flood, a flood of bodies, a
flood in the crosswalk. Yes, Black liberation
ahora ngayon na. Yes, middle class youth
duct-taping handwritten cardboard signs
to their new Hyundais & rapping the fuck
out of "Fuck tha Police." Show me
anti-imperialism. Show me all of it.
Show me this historiography of feeling:
Black & brown families, refugees &
migrants, lining the avenue during this
caravan protest because they
know so intimately the surveillance,
the threat. They know so intimately
that such terrors are routine. If we suspend
the need to be practical, we become
neighbors against & outside of state.
Some poetics pretend a non-rhetoric to
let language do its own work, & in such
pretending these poetics remove poetics
as a work doing work in the form &
content of wake, of tattered trash bag
capital, chewed-up water bottle caps, Abolition
Now! pins & perfectly inflated birthday
balloons. Teach me to fight against
ethnographic impulse, to cancel the
descriptive, the snapshot, the spectacle,
the grace of rigorous solitude. I may be
super annoyed, but something super is
happening next door—a youth gamer is

screaming at his screen: Fuck tha police, Bro!
& yes yes, Bro, show me hella Muslim cabbies
& protest medics double-parking their
Priuses & sedans outside the mosque
at the mouth of this alley.

These embodied vacancies, these disassembled
obliterations, these dark poems of an other, these
parking lot nail salons, these crowds on University
& Euclid, these eucalyptus ointments, these
sufferings establish a radical angst of manifesto.
This is not about political stakes. It's hardly about how
high they've become, how rough the study & struggle,
how holistic the gathered assembly, how transitory the
sadness; rather, this is about church feeling, about lived
intensities of interior traffic that are so depleting, so returned,
so disinterested in a randomness of light, they incline
toward these irresistible graffitis.

so that I may invent my lungs

— AIMÉ CÉSAIRE

call this radicalized grief

call this rigorous animality

call this divine sorrow

We believe the world to be temporary. We are
always nervous about what lives between work

& the work of suicide. We believe in aftermath
of disaster, light to heavy, charred geography

where we are less ourselves & still somewhat
in love. We have heard rumors about this city—

the awe, the result, gentrification waking up publics,
heavy with liquor, the alluded-to dead searching for

fragments we've wept. Today, Ziploc bags of
overused surgical masks & spare change: wakes

by the river, scripted rumors about this city. We
keep secrets of cousins, & come to know aunties,

an impossible other: tilapia & tamarind, hair under
water, recently released homie in transit, on a

curb, in velvet, freezing, homie's home now bus
stop benches. Allegedly, we are the ones who

have crucified sun, this water. & the neighborhood
now smells half-eaten. There lacks prophecy in

the sound of migrants being brutalized. Call aunties,
call uncles for space on their apartment floors!

Call aunties, call uncles for green cards! Call aunties,
call uncles for family! This morning stabbed in

robbery. Aunties & uncles collect night smoke—
always a mist, popular, an opening. We play a history

of hiding aunties hiding uncles, sleepless cousins
of refusal, the refuse under the deep of this city.

in which there is no innovating
loss in which dead batteries

flatten under the weight of car
in which I ask for nothing but

to live in this suffering in which
skull itself throbs against baton

in which history is murky in
which we murk history the ways

in which these deliverances happen:
I have not a desire but a need to be

this nobody who knows no one
or nothing on the way to nowhere

Aesthetic of intellect beneath hands,

hands beneath running water, running

water a woman, a woman singing,

a singing woman a singed cartography.

You are here to disarticulate body

from voice, a material dilemma—yes,

so singular. You demand prose that

stains heart, a hand that fails form.

You, thorough haunting, dried mud

in your fingernails, are here tonight.

& tonight, let children run, let

them gently tear into the sky, let

them imagine, too, what it is to be

torn through a lyric of expired want.

It is said that Homeboy tried to stand after his Harley slammed into the truck.

This is about how temporality becomes collapsed griefscape.

You wish to reimagine that scene: Homeboy, in a brown & black Pendleton, a clean white T, pressed Ben Davis khakis, Chucks, black locs, cruising down Oceanside Blvd.

You & the others wait at the corner of Oceanside & Crouch.

You can hear the faint hum of Homeboy's Harley approaching.

The family—kids, lolas, lolos, aunties, uncles, cousins, all wearing T-shirts with Homeboy's picture on it, red & black Ifugao-patterned cloth wrapped around their waists, white socks pulled up tight, & Chucks real clean.

Homeboy's father, in a barong, & denim vest, & long Dickie's shorts, & Chucks, too, is singing along to a video of Homeboy drunkenly reciting Keith Urban's "Blue Ain't Your Color."

On the sidewalk is a cardboard box overflowing with dried roses, tulips, & carnations.

You & the cousins & the homies are toasting, downing the deadliest of mixes—one shot Patron, one shot Maker's Mark, & one shot 151: Galvatron.

You pour some out on the sidewalk.

Someone lights the sidewalk on fire.

Those with bikes rev the hell out of their engines.

You hear nothing but the revving & Homeboy's father singing, Homeboy's mother crying.

But Homeboy is coming through.

You hear his Harley approaching.

You see Homeboy, his locs, his smile.

As Homeboy passes, he nods what-up & turns right on Crouch & rides up the mountain forever & ever.

See the aunties dance, see the lolas dance, see the little ones dance.

& dance & dance.

Let us begin this world
anew. I build this fort with

pillows, blankets, bed sheets,
dining chairs, stacks of
therapy books, ethnic studies
books, binder clips, & tiny
clothespins. This is a house party
invented for two. We are here
to make the unthinkable
necessary. The air conditioner
blows even colder under here.
We reckon with restless ghosts
under here. We demand nothing
less than the recklessness of
memory, the autonomy of sorrow,
& these counter-narratives of joy.

Here is a parable,
a prayer, perhaps,
for those unmapped:

Here are new students
considering new lives,
new interrogations, new
footnotes, but no new
friendships, no news. None.

Still, the problem of loans.

Still, the problem of rent.

Still, the problem of property.

This alley off University is
a gallery of abandoned mattresses
stacked against limp wire fencing that
leans against wood panels that

shade the driveway where the
unmapped fall asleep.

Ancestral spirits are
no less spectacle than
principled remembrance:

The craft of this tissue
we often call ourselves.

you & I desire nothing short of the unthinkable
you & I desire nothing short of the unthinkable
you & I desire nothing short of the unthinkable
you & I desire nothing short of the unthinkable
you & I desire nothing short of the unthinkable
you & I desire nothing short of the unthinkable
you & I desire nothing short of the unthinkable
you & I desire nothing short of the unthinkable
you & I desire nothing short of the unthinkable
you & I desire nothing short of the unthinkable
you & I desire nothing short of the unthinkable
you & I desire nothing short of the unthinkable
you & I desire nothing short of the unthinkable
you & I desire nothing short of the unthinkable

                                        invention of failure
                                            failure of maybe

maybe of project
    project of surplus

                                        surplus of forever
                                            forever of play

play of distance
    distance of regard

                                        regard of worth
                                            worth of excess

excess of pretext
    pretext of pause

                                        pause of return
                                            return of land

after you revolt you return you mute
make permutations of afterlife same
shipfire fabulous same antagonism

same dawning same graffitied prayer
same thick gesture such solidarity such
concrete bus rider monologue mark such

lawless friendship whose blood stays
tenement fire whose laughter melts
marrow whose vigor whose intention

whose lungs whose regard for whom
poetics seems refusal seems worth it
worth this traffic this devalued affinity

toward an exacting neverness of capital
of nothing of nobody of nowhere a citation
of estranged body on non-propertied space for

words run amok words run rampant words
against rampart words against borders words
for what we do for what has been done to us

to make mourning to scratch this lit
architecture this swapmeet splendor slack
burden blow blow this unbuilt history

you & I fake rare confidence
you & I train strange analytic
you & I ghost backfire migrations
you & I exhaust calm faith
you & I tense firecracker past
you & I break lack syntax
you & I grammar this turn
you & I tender such rapture
you & I sweet talk geography
you & I monster most futurity
you & I compute lost glory
you & I wildfire soliloquy
you & I flea market friendly
you & I wreck what archive

I ask about what falls away.

I ask about where water sings.

Here is surplus of sun, ocean

of excess, remaindered song.

Whose hands wash this sky?

Who drains this sun against worry?

Whose mighty ache makes history?

This is where water drains,

where gardens grow against

worry, against the throb & rot,

& the throb & rot knows nothing but

the veil hiding hand from profit. Here

is leftover rice. & the wild imaginary

of hunger. Here is a canal in

the crook of the earth. & here is

where water sings. & this, this

is water singing us elsewhere.

WE DRAFT WORK SONGS FOR THIS CITY:
A REMIX

whenever we stretch grammars of worry past the Pacific
whenever another blackout gifts us much needed stillness

whenever the surrender of this quiet is typhoon enough we
draft work songs for this city mighty we of rough draft

futures mighty we in river-mouth of rush hour traffic we
of protest chant & scrapyard syntax we draft on the corner

of Black Mountain & Mira Mesa here on a sidewalk of torn
shoelaces & lost grocery lists we draft blueprints for survival

we survive on the smell of beef broth the smell of basil of
turmeric of cilantro of carne asada of freshly cooked rice

of steamed bok choy of freshwater fish of deep-fried rice
paper we work song at this bus stop for students we work

song at this bus stop for tech workers this bus stop for lolas
y abuelitas we work song in tin drum glottal syllables of

distant motherlands we draft litanies at every streetlight
altar we draft verse on napkins & reused plastic grocery

bags wherever there are elders playing chess & waxing
geographic outside the donut shop whenever much needed

stillness promises a new hour whenever the Pacific knows
to rupture the shoreline whenever typhoon is fractal hum in

chest we draft work songs for this city we raw material
literatures we distillation of afterdreams we swapmeet

philosophers we draft work songs on the corner of Genesee
& Clairemont Mesa we draft gutters scattered with pink

boba straws & dried palm leaves we draft for mothers & children
hustling bouquets of carnations from the bicycle lane we draft

for parolees in orange vests selling local tribunes from the center
island we draft on Murray Ridge where a family sells roses &

chocolate from a white bucket whenever the small hour calls
collect whenever ruptures in the line set us free whenever hum

in chest arrives as ghost in throat we draft work songs we whose
hands wash sky we who grow gardens & gardens against worry

we whose mighty ache remakes history we draft work songs here
in the alley off University behind 49th we draft a perfectly

reusable red plastic slide a car full of birthday balloons a
small hill of middle grade paperbacks a gold purse full of fresh

broccoli & rubber gloves a black tote bag stuffed with wet lettuce
& white surgical masks we draft at the backyard family parties

& block-wide barbecues we work song where it smells of fresh
tires & flour tortillas where dried lemon rinds stick to pavement

work song of cleaned chicken bone wrapped in foil work song of
rainsoaked boxsprings work song for the infamous hot cheetos

burrito brushfire fabulous work song work song on the graveyard
shift survivor song song of the parking lot nail salon work song

of the underfuture heavenly pho outside between two buildings
work song we draft as patrol cars cram the alley we draft as protest

medics cram the alley we draft as Muslim cabbies double-park their
Priuses outside the mosque outside the taqueria work song of a child

chasing mosquitos with a hammer wherever a community of uncles
gathers in the shared parking lot of the banh mi shop & Somali

restaurant wherever we feel that lived intensity of interior traffic here
sings the lettuce-picker here sings the strawberry-picker here sings

the bellhop the postal worker the custodian the hotel maid grounds-
keeper landscaper gardener construction worker nurse teacher waiter

dishwasher bus driver grocer labor organizer mechanic therapist here
sings the nanny here sings the refugee here sings the Native here sings

the migrant O, what work! O, what song! O, what city! when our utterance
is archive when there is historical reckoning when we demand nothing

short of collective joy & here we are on Native land we draft work songs for
this city we draft work songs for this city we draft work songs for this city

NOTES

p. 9: This epigraph is from Neferti X. M. Tadiar, *Things Fall Away: Philippine Historical Experience and the Making of Globalization* (Durham: Duke University Press, 2009), 14.

p. 12: The phrase "fish-hooks of hope" is sampled from Aimé Césaire, *Return to My Native Land*, trans. John Berger and Anna Bostock (Brooklyn, NY: Archipelago, 2014), 9. The reference to "kitchen table" politics is inspired by Barbara Smith and Beverly Smith, "Across the Kitchen Table: A Sister-to-Sister Dialogue," in *This Bridge Called My Back: Writings by Radical Women of Color*, 4th Edition, edited by Cherríe Moraga and Gloria Anzaldúa (Albany, NY: SUNY Press, 2015), 111-125. The phrase "restless ghosts" is sampled from Lisa Marie Cacho, *Social Death: Racialized Rightlessness and the Criminalization of the Unprotected* (New York: NYU Press, 2012), 168.

pp. 16-20: The phrase "in the shadow of capital" is sampled from Lisa Lowe and David Lloyd, "Introduction," *The Politics of Culture in the Shadow of Capital*, edited by Lisa Lowe and David Lloyd (Durham: Duke University Press, 1997), 1-32; the notion of "Abomunist" is from Bob Kaufman, "Abomunist Manifesto," Poets.org, Academy of American Poets; to be clear, the relational assemblage of protest chants here holds the tensions inherent in the specificity and temporality of geographically disparate struggles, in other words, 'land back,' 'deoccupy,' and 'demilitarize,' all refer to the movement to Free Palestine, and to a move toward genuine solidarity with Kumeyaay peoples and lands, Luiseño/Payómkawichum peoples and lands, but also to principled solidarity with all peoples and all lands subjected to ongoing colonial and settler colonial violence. The phrase "this throb this / rot of racial capitalism" is instructed by Daniel Borzutsky's phrase "rotten carcass economy" in *The Performance of Becoming Human* (New York: Brooklyn Arts Press, 2016), 32.

p. 23: The phrase "Such mourning is discontinuous" is inspired by the sentence "What I find utterly terrifying is mourning's discontinuous character," in Roland Barthes, *Mourning Diary*, trans. Richard Howard (New York: Hill and Wang, 2012), 67.

pp. 25-27: This narrative attempt is in memory of Brendon Benito (1977-2019).

p. 28: The phrase "breath of inexhaustible thought" is sampled from Aimé Césaire, *Return to My Native Land*, trans. John Berger and Anna Bostock (Brooklyn, NY: Archipelago, 2014), 9.

p. 31: This epigraph is from Claudia Rankine, *Don't Let Me Be Lonely* (Saint Paul: Graywolf Press, 2004), 120.

p. 87: This epigraph is from Neferti X. M. Tadiar, *Things Fall Away: Philippine Historical Experience and the Making of Globalization* (Durham: Duke University Press, 2009), 370.

pp. 89-91: This anthem is in memory of writer, activist, and super-mentor Susan F. Quimpo (1961-2020). For more about Ate Susan and her family, please read Susan F. Quimpo and Nathan Gilbert Quimpo, *Subversive Lives: A Family Memoir of the Marcos Years* (Athens: Ohio University Press, 2016).

p. 92: The keywords here index a range of ethnic studies and ethnic studies-adjacent scholarship. For instance, the notion of the "remaindered" is conceptualized in Neferti X. M. Tadiar, "Decolonization, 'Race,' and Remaindered Life Under Empire," in *Critical Ethnic Studies: A Reader*, edited by Critical Ethnic Studies Editorial Collective (Durham: Duke University Press, 2016), 395-415; the subjectivities and qualities of the "fugitive" is in conversation with Fred Moten and Stefano Harney, *The Undercommons: Fugitive Planning & Black Study* (Brooklyn, NY: Minor Compositions, 2013); the "haunted" is derived from Avery F. Gordon, *Ghostly Matters: Haunting and the Sociological Imagination* (Minneapolis: University of Minnesota Press, 1997); and the "unprotected" subject—accompanied by a crucial theorization of value—is deepened in Lisa Marie Cacho, *Social Death: Racialized Rightlessness and the Criminalization of the Unprotected* (New York: NYU Press, 2012).

pp. 93-94: This rewrite of a Catholic litany is inspired by the litanies in R. Zamora Linmark, *Rolling the R's* (New York: Kaya Press, 1995), 28-33.

pp. 95-98: This distillation is primarily in memory of Arcadio Perez (1937-2018).

p. 100: The imagery of the "cranial guitar" is a nod to Bob Kaufman, *Cranial Guitar* (Minneapolis: Coffee House Press, 1995).

p. 103: The phrases and remixes of "rhythm of suffering" and "I know now that my mourning will be chaotic" are sampled from Roland Barthes, *Mourning Diary*, trans. Richard Howard (New York: Hill and Wang, 2012), 162 and 31, respectively.

pp. 104-106: Some text here is sampled, cut-up, and rearranged from Robin D. G. Kelley, "Why We Won't Wait," *CounterPunch*, counterpunch.org, November 25, 2014, and David Hernandez et al., "San Diego police fatally shoot man they say pointed gun at officers," *San Diego Union Tribune*, sandiegotribune.com, July 9, 2020. The caravan protest described here took place on June 6, 2020. Protestors drove from various sites with histories of police violence—e.g. La Jolla, City Heights, National City, Donovoan State Prison. BLM San Diego narrated via Facebook Live on issues such as violence against Black women, the impact of gentrification in Hillcrest on the Black queer and trans community, and the intimacies between immigrant detention and police violence against Black folks. The phrasing "If we suspend the need to be practical" is sampled from Lisa Marie Cacho, *Social Death: Racialized Rightlessness and the Criminalization of the Unprotected* (New York: NYU Press, 2012), 31. There is a humble nod here to what Christina Sharpe conceptualizes as 'wake work.' In describing 'wake work' as an analytic, Sharpe writes: "we might continue to imagine new ways to live in the wake of slavery, in slavery's afterlives, to survive (and more) the afterlife of property." For future study, I'm interested in thinking through these 'new ways to live' relationally and across differently situated analytics and historical contexts—i.e. 'wake work' and what Neferti X. M. Tadiar calls 'remaindered life' (see above)—in order to identify new/alternative forms of subjectivity and solidarity. See Christina Sharpe, *In the Wake: On Blackness and Being* (Durham: Duke University Press, 2016), 18.

p. 109: This epigraph is from Aimé Césaire, *Return to My Native Land*, trans. John Berger and Anna Bostock (Brooklyn, NY: Archipelago, 2014), 78.

p. 111: The phrases "radicalized grief" and "divine sorrow" are sampled from Neferti X. M. Tadiar, *Things Fall Away: Philippine Historical Experience and the Making of Globalization* (Durham: Duke University Press, 2009), 15, 376, 378, respectively.

p. 114: The sentence "There is no innovating loss" is sampled from Claudia Rankine, *Don't Let Me Be Lonely* (Saint Paul: Graywolf Press, 2004), 57. The sentence "I ask for nothing but to live in this suffering" and the fragment "I have not a desire but a need" is sampled from Roland Barthes, *Mourning Diary*, trans. Richard Howard (New York: Hill and Wang, 2012), 174 and 91, respectively.

pp. 117-118: This reimagined scene is in memory of Clark Domilos (1983-2018).

pp. 119-120: This excerpt samples and reprocesses the following sentence: "To make the unthinkable not just plausible but necessary, we have to reckon with restless ghosts and living people who share the status of dead-to-others and demand from us nothing less than transformation" from Lisa Marie Cacho, *Social Death: Racialized Rightlessness and the Criminalization of the Unprotected* (New York: NYU Press, 2012), 168.

p. 121: The phrase "a prayer, perhaps" refers to the notion of 'divine sorrow' and is sampled from Neferti X. M. Tadiar, *Things Fall Away: Philippine Historical Experience and the Making of Globalization* (Durham: Duke University Press, 2009), 378.

pp. 123-127: This polyptych samples, reconfigures, and draws its critical energy from the following lines, fragments, and sentences: "To be born to the world is an exhausting splendor", "For, it's all the same: the same fire", "The one who, at dawn, and while the fogs thicken the gesture, makes the first sign of friendship", and "I write far from my house, to return to it safe, to gain its concrete flesh, distance" from Édouard Glissant, *Sun of Consciousness*, trans. Nathanaël (New York: Nightboat Books, 2020), 16, 38, 69, 48, respectively; "I play / revolted midnight always / coming back", "The burden can be muted", "history of the unbuilt project, what it documents / of the blow it up, / history of the push", "I'm trying to write the poetry of riding the bus in the city", and "There might be only a few folks for whom the poems seem worth it (not in spite of but because of their failure or refusal to communicate)" from Fred Moten, *B Jenkins* (Durham: Duke University Press, 2010), 38, 48, 74, 105, 104, respectively; "the same woman whose blood is full of tenement fire", "so you find nothing / so you find nobody", "That evening, that moment, that forever, that exact never, my laughter melts my lungs", "Where & when & how is it that we have come to do what we do with little or no regard to what has been done to us?", and "If I scratched with vigor & intention, could I disappear?" from Jason Magabo Perez, *This is for the mostless* (Cincinnati: WordTech Editions, 2017), 31, 39, 91, 22, 110, respectively; "produce a new analytics through which to apprehend co-alitional possibilities, or in other words 'strange affinities'", "is to invent a politics", "must traffic in the unknowable and the devalued", and "Co-alition in this context would therefore mean a confederation of discrete formations" from Grace Kyungwon Hong and Roderick A. Ferguson, eds., *Strange Affinities: The Gender and Sexual Politics of Comparative Racialization* (Durham: Duke University Press, 2011), 18, 12, 16, 8, respectively; "What is at stake in taking up this all too rare opportunity to pause, to think, and to play with words the possibility of imagining a nonproper-tied space of decolonial knowledge production", and "In other words, we must write words that run amuck/amok" from Sarita Echavez See, *The Filipino Primitive: Accumulation and Resistance in the American Museum* (New York: NYU Press, 2017), 18 and 19, respectively.

p. 128: This lyric is written after Philip Vera Cruz, "Profits Enslave the World," in Craig Scharlin and Lilia Villanueva, *Philip Vera Cruz: A Personal History of Filipino Immigrants and the Farmworkers Movement*, 3rd Edition (Seattle: University of Washington Press, 2000), 2.

pp. 129-132: This remix includes fragments and revisions from the long poem preceding it. It was composed for Mayor Todd Gloria's San Diego State of the City Address on January 11, 2023 at the San Diego Civic Theatre in San Diego, California.

pp. 141-142: Professor Tadiar discusses 'the mostless' as explored in Jason Magabo Perez, *This is for the mostless* (Cincinnati: WordTech Editions, 2017). References to a specific lyric by José Garcia Villa is from *José Garcia Villa, Doveglion: Collected Poems* (New York: Penguin, 2008), 47.

HERE WE ARE: AN AFTERWORD
NEFERTI X. M. TADIAR

Here we are.

It is the end of the third year of a global pandemic, two decades of intensified global war and finance, a century of U.S. empire, and half a millennium of colonial capitalist rule, and Jason Magabo Perez asks about what falls away. In a time when the dominant protocols for saving life continue to depend on and intensify racial capitalist structures of valuation, entailing the shedding of lives deemed essential only insofar as they uphold and protect the valued life they serve; in a time when the rush to a new normal of institutionalized emergency rule is only outstripped by the pace of events beyond human compass or control; in this time, which is as recent and present as it is centuries long, to ask about what falls away is to give us pause, to catch our belabored breath, to mourn losses only quietly grieved, to reckon with "restless ghosts / archived in [your] veins," a sadness of lives continuously shorn of their own incommensurable beauty. It is a sadness that we have yet to reckon with, a sadness that is willfully forgotten or diminished yet remains the repository of our deepest and most radical prayers.

In this poetic vein, in the vein of parable and prayer, Perez asks about all that we know is cast out and that we are yearning to retrieve or remember, for it is what and who we are—the we to whom and from where he writes, the we he first gathered and honored in his debut book of prose poetry under the canopy of the "mostless." "Mostly are we mostless, / And neverness is all we become" is the José Garcia Villa epigraph of that earlier book, This is for the mostless, a beautiful and moving collection of humorous-sad memorial tributes to the author's immigrant Filipino community of childhood selves and pop heroes, homies and family, aunts and nephews, mother and grandmother, and friends and lovers, living and loving in the shadows and motley light of a traumatic racial-izing American dream. In the poem by Villa, from which these opening lines were drawn, the fate of ontological voidance or dispossessed being ("The tiger is tigerless / The flame is flameless") gives way to the self's divine resurrection and immortality. In Perez's collection, remembrances of those fated for neverness restore and celebrate the bodies and the pathos and joy of their mundane strivings, their clumsy attempts to be and be loved. Remembrances become the form of a holy communion in which we might partake.

Here we are returned to the mostless, to a we of without, a we that has become as expansive as it is intimate. The broad descriptors have multiplied, indicating the many forms of expulsion and privation, which the untrammeled global pursuit of wealth and supremacy requires, that make for the 'we' defined by paradoxical proximity and distance to a superlative condition, by a fate of ever-unrealized or foreclosed being. Perez asks about savage and salvaged, surplussed and remaindered, monstrous and fugitive, excess and haunted, hunted and precarious, unmapped and unprotected, mostless and underfuture. Many of these are the terms of a growing body of critical and creative work in Black, postcolonial, and ethnic studies and cultures. They are concepts and names for social experiences on the part of peoples who have histori-cally borne the violence of colonial and imperial projects and continue to suffer the greatest consequences as well as life costs of those con-temporary systems in the present-day. Asking about these assignations, Perez glimpses singular and plural persons, a formidable yet unseen agency of worldly caring work, work of pain and creation:

> Whose hands wash this sky?

> Who drains this sun against worry?

> Whose mighty ache makes history?

To ask about is also to look for and to look after—to attend to, to care for—the unmentioned and unmapped who comprise this planetary force. Despite its role in maintaining this world as we know it, this force of people—wanting, working, desiring— appears as merely the detritus of global ideals and achievements; they appear as devalued, disposable lives everywhere abounding without sufficient political or historical reckoning.

I ask about what falls away is an elegy and praise poem for these lives lived in ache and dereliction, lives of Black, brown, refugee and migrant communities in neighborhoods of Southern California. It mourns and remembers the intimate geography of their sometimes serviceable, always waiting, laboring lives traced in their scattered leavings of receipts and grocery lists on sidewalks, lingering smells of ethnic food and fuel by bus stops, and the familiar glottal stops and sounds of "un-English languages" in the air. Here amidst the life traces of the foreclosure and fallout of loans, rent, property—of lands, neighborhoods, and houses folded into new racial capitalist schemes of investment and dispossession, conscription and abandonment—we find a sadness and loneliness borne by those for whom it is a historical fate and political praxis of protest and refusal. Here sadness is "its own godforsaken solidarity statement," an anticolonial and abolitionist sadness reaching out across the different languages and social terrains of radical liberation movements across the world.

For how can we not be filled with sadness, with the leftovers of lives, others and our own, that will not add up to something—the litter of lifetimes used up and discarded, like coffee napkins in an old entry model car and bodily scars, which Perez reads as "scars from a life of being worked"? But in making a place of recollection of the scraps of connected lives and losses, a place of gathering for the disassembly of the salvaged among these masses of sadness (the masses of messianic power), Perez offers us glimpses of fleeting joy, of kinship and belonging, of ways of living and singing that take place nevertheless in the crevices and alleyways in the forlorn landscapes of a "charred geography." We are allowed dreams of transformation in the direction of oceanic fullness: "surplus of sun, ocean / of excess, remaindered song." What falls away from our articulated political ideals are these litanies of mourning and survival, which are also the craft of our social being, our anthems of promise.

Here we are. It is fact and entreaty. It is defiance and affirmation. Prelude to uprising. Collective song.

ACKNOWLEDGMENTS

Many big thanks to the generous editors, curators, and organizers of the following publications, platforms, and venues for their time, care, and labor in publishing excerpts from this work: *Academy of American Poets* (Poets.org); *Kalfou: A Journal of Comparative and Relational Ethnic Studies*; *Marías at Sampaguitas*; *San Diego Poetry Annual*; *Sonora Review*; *TLDTD*; *The Operating System*; *Community Building Art Works (CBAW) Anthology*; *Persistence and Rupture* by The REEF Project; *Read Ritual: An Anthology* by Locked Horn Press; *CSUSM News Center*; *San Diego Union-Tribune*; *UC San Diego Magazine*; *Profits Enslave the World*, a virtual exhibition by the Bulosan Center for Filipino Studies and Welga Archive; Progressive Labor Summit; Writing on the Wall Festival in Liverpook UK; Center for Art and Thought (CA+T); and NPR's *Here & Now*.

...

I offer my sincerest, most infinite, and most humblest gratitude to you, yes you, to all of you who have lifted me in your most loving and most mostless ways, to all of you who have helped hold and carry this grief and this joy, to all of you who already know what it is: the loveliest, the love of my life, my bestest friend, my kasama-confidant; my parents; my brothers; my sisters; all my beautiful, imaginative, and intelligent nieces and nephews; mga inaanak ko; my dear cousins; my aunties; my uncles; my lolos; my lolas; my dearest homies across all lands, all oceans; mga kasama ko/mis compas; and all past and present students and mentors.

I stay humbled and honored to be in community with those poets who have participated and shared in the daily experiments within The Digital Sala grind(s): Butch Schwarzkopf; Christian Aldana; Czaerra Galicinao Ucol; David Maduli; Eunice Andrada; Hari Alluri; Janice Lobo Sapigao;

Keana Aguila Labra; Liaa Melissa Fernandez; Maria Bolaños; Michelle Peñaloza; and Rachelle Cruz. Many thanks, too, to those whose feedback, insights, and intellectual comradeship were super present during this series of emotional-intellectual exercises: Alden Sajor Marte-Wood; Alexandra Cavallaro; Amrah Salómon J.; Arash Haile; Barbara Jane Reyes; Charlene Martinez; C. Ree; Denise Pacheco; Dianne Que; Jasmine Lee; Jennifer Derilo; Josen Masangkay Diaz; K. Wayne Yang; Lea Johnson; Le-Keisha Hughes; Leslie Quintanilla; Malathi Iyengar; Maisam Alomar; May Fu; Monica Batac; Natchee Blu Barnd; Patrick Anderson; R. Xach Williams; Rashaan Alexis Meneses; Thea Quiray Tagle; Vineeta Singh; Yumi Pak; and Zeinabu Davis.

I'm grateful to have been gifted a timely virtual residency during the Spring of 2020 with the beloved, inimitable, and forever missed digital giant, Center for Art and Thought (CA+T): Thank you, Sarita See, mads lê, and Clare Counihan, for the space, time, and encouragement to reimagine and reignite a praxis of writing against accumulation.

Much gratitude to those who supported the initial virtual performance of this work: Lucy Mae San Pablo Burns and the Pilipino Studies Minor in the Department of Asian American Studies at UCLA and Robyn Rodriguez and Wayne Jopanda at the Bulosan Center for Filipino Studies for helping host the event; Ka-Bang Lauron for your gorgeous artwork and design; Czaerra for Zoom security; Hari and Christian for helping bring voice to this experiment; Susana Parras and Alex Villalpando for your expansively gentle and generative verbal foreword and afterword—the container—of the performance.

I remain indebted to and instructed by the writing, thinking, and labor of Neferti Tadiar—thank you, Professor Tadiar, for helping us all find ways to look for each other in remaindered space and time, and maraming salamat for your beautiful meditation in the afterword.

I'd like to especially thank the following poets for your generous reading and insight: Angela Peñaredondo; Hari Alluri; Maryam Ivette Parhizkar; Muriel Leung; Rachelle Cruz; Sandra Doller; Sesshu Foster; and Vejea Jennings.

Thank you, Matt Manalo, for lending your stunning artwork for the book cover. And thank you, Chez Bryan Ong, for capturing in the design the threshold between what holds and what falls away.

This book arrives during the second year of my term as San Diego Poet Laureate, and I'm grateful to the San Diego Commission for Arts and Culture for their continued support. In particular, thank you, Lara Bullock and Christine Jones, for your continued guidance and encouragement.

I'm so deeply thrilled to have this book published by the visionary Kaya Press—so very many thanks to Neelanjana Banerjee and Sunyoung Lee for your careful and caring vision and enthusiasm for this book, its communities, and its futures.

ABOUT THE AUTHOR

Jason Magabo Perez serves as San Diego Poet Laureate 2023-24. Perez is the author of *Phenomenology of Superhero* (Red Bird Chapbooks, 2016), *This is for the mostless* (WordTech Editions, 2017), and *I ask about what falls away* (Kaya Press, 2024). Perez's work has appeared in *Interim*, *Witness*, *The Feminist Wire*, *Marías at Sampaguitas*, *TLDTD*, *San Diego Union-Tribune*, NPR's *Here & Now*, among others. Recipient of a Challenge America Grant from the National Endowment for the Arts, previous Artist-in-Residence at the Center for Art and Thought, and current Poet Laureate Fellow with Academy of American Poets, Perez has performed at notable venues such as the National Asian American Theater Festival, International Conference of the Philippines, Yerba Buena Center for the Arts, La Jolla Playhouse, and Los Angeles Contemporary Exhibitions. Perez serves as a core organizer of The Digital Sala and as an Associate Editor at Ethnic Studies Review. Perez is an Associate Professor of Ethnic Studies at California State University San Marcos.